THE BABYLONIAN CAPTIVITY

by
Lesya Ukrainka
(Лариса Петрівна Косач-Квітка)

Mudborn Press

The Bablyonian Captivity © 2014 Mudborn Press

ISBN 978-0-930012-52-6

LITERARY FICTION

Family Secret, Last American Housewife, Period Pieces, Eleanore Hill
Aurora Leigh, E.B. Browning   Hadji Murad, Tolstoy   The Basement,
Newborn The First Detective. Poe   Matilda, Mary Shelley

SPECULATIVE FICTION

Frankenstein, Mary Shelley   The Martian Testament, Sasha Newborn

HISTORY

Mitos y Leyendas/Myths and Legends of Mexico   Ossian Legends
Beechers Through the 19th Century   Uncle Tom's Cabin, H. B. Stowe

SCHOOLING

Don't Panic: Procrastinator's Guide to Writing an Effective Term Paper
First Person Intense   Italian for Opera Lovers
French for Food Lovers Doctorese for the imPatient

SPIRITUAL

Ghazals of Ghalib   Gandhi on the *Bhagavad Gita*
Gospel According to Tolstoy   Everlasting Gospel, William Blake

LOVE

Dante & His Circle   Vita Nuova   Sappho Dickens, Christmas Carol

STAGING SHAKESPEARE

DIRECTOR'S PLAYBOOK SERIES: Hamlet   Merchant of Venice
Twelfth Night   Taming of the Shrew   Midsummer Night's Dream
Romeo and Juliet As You Like It Richard III Henry V Much Ado About
Nothing Macbeth Othello Julius Caesar King Lear Antony and Cleopatra

7 Plays / Transgender Characters   Falstaff: 4 Plays Venus and Adonis

TEACHERS ONLY

(*Q & A, glossaries, critical comments*)
Areopagitica, John Milton   Apology of Socrates, & Crito, Plato
Leaves of Grass, Walt Whitman   Sappho, The Poems

Introduction

This poetic drama of the Jews in exile in Babylon, by the major poet and activist of her time Lesya Ukrainka, was nothing less than an allegory of the oppressed Ukrainian population under the domination of the Russian Empire in the late Nineteenth Century. Ukrainka was a leader in the Literary and Artistic Society, which was banned for its support for Ukrainian nationalism. In order to publish her first book of poetry in the Ukrainian language (forbidden where she lived), she sent it to Kiev to be published under the pseudonym Lesya Ukrainka. She died just over one hundred years ago, yet her passion for Ukrainian independence from Russian control continues to motivate the population of Ukraine.

This translation, based on the 1916 work of C. Bechhofer, is modernized for today's readers.

Sasha Newborn
August 2014

§

*(A wide plain. The red sunset turns
the waters of the Euphrates to blood.
Scattered on the plain are seen the tents
of the Hebrew captives. Naked children
seek shells in the mud and gather
brushwood for the fires. Weary women,
mostly old, in rags, are busied preparing
supper, each at her own hearth, for
the men that have just returned from
the town after their toil and are sitting
silently under the willows near the water.
A little farther off, also under the willows,
stand two groups, the Levites and the
prophets. On the willows, over the
prophets' heads, harps hang; quivering
from time to time, they jingle in the
evening wind. Far away are seen the walls
and towers of Babylon and sometimes
there comes the noise of the city.)*

§

§

A Woman (at her fire): Husband, come to supper.

> (*A man, still young, leaves a group and silently sits down.*)

Woman: Why do you not eat bread? (*The man is silent.*) Is it bitter? There is nothing to be done, poor thing, you must eat.

The Man: (*mumbling like an old man*) I cannot eat.

Woman: Misery! Have you no teeth? Where...

Man: There ! (*points to Babylon.*)

Woman: Misery, misery, misery !

§

§

(An Old Man approaches an old woman sitting by the extinguished fire of another hearth, motionless, her head bowed down)

Old Man: Give me supper ! (*The woman is silent and motionless.*) Why haven't you prepared it? (*The woman is silent.*) Why do you have ashes on your hair? (*The woman is silent, and bows still lower.*) Where is our daughter?

The Old Woman: There!

> (*points to Babylon and pours ashes upon her head.*)

Old Man: Adonai!

> (*Tears his garments and falls down.*)

§

§

*(At a third fire sit only men, mostly old.
A woman approaches timidly; ragged
children hang at her garments.)*

The Woman: My fathers, pardon that I ask you;
   have you not seen my husband?

An Old Man: How is he called?

The Woman: Ebenezer of Ossia.

Another Old Man: Was he so called before you were
   a widow?

The Woman: What are you saying?

A Third Old Man: Do not kill yourself! Foes do not
   torment the dead.

The Woman: What shall I do—miserable—with my
   little children?

The Children: Mother, mother, mother!

§

§

A Mad Woman: (*wandering among the fires*) Happy the womb that did not bear; happy the breast that gave not suck. Hey! rejoice not, Babylonian woman! Hey! be not glad, mother of vipers' sons!

A Girl: (*whispers to her companion, pointing at the mad woman*): It's from the time her child was killed in Jerusalem.

Companion: How terrible!

Girl: And I saw it with my own eyes, how the soldier seized her boy by his feet and struck at...

Companion: Be silent!

§

§

The Levites: (*under the willows*) For our fathers'
    sin the Lord took from us the temple; for our
    ancestors' dishonor He took away His church.
    And now, as a spendthrift's children, innocent
    we expiate our fathers' debt.

The Prophets: Jerusalem smote us with stones,
    and for it the wrath of the Lord smote her. The
    daughter of Zion despised us, and for it the son
    of Baal subdued her.

First Levite: (*to another*) Why have you not been at
    prayers?

Second Levite: The master sent me to the
    reckonings. The workmen from Haram are being
    paid for their labor at the king's palace.

First Levite: Could you not find one of the scribes
    to take your place?

Second Levite: Service, brother! The master says no
    men are so skilled at reckoning as the Hebrews.

First Levite: True.

Second Levite: (*aside to him*) For my good help the
    chief gave me this ring.

First Levite: Glory to the Lord, that He hath distinguished His people by wisdom above the nations of all the world. (*Aside*) Is there no need of another to help?

(*They whisper.*)

§

§

A Samarian Prophet: Thus spake the Lord: On
  Garisim I have built an abode, on its summit I
  made My altar, but you forsook it and knew not
  the house of My glory, as the foolish bibbing son
  knows not his father's abode and wanders in
  outer darkness, a butt for strangers' children.

A Jewish Prophet: Thus spake the Lord: In
  Jerusalem I made My abode among the people,
  that, as bees come together to one hive, to one
  queen, so would you come together unto Me, to
  the only Temple; but, as a wild swarm, you flew
  away, and for it I sent evil hornets against you.

Samarian Prophet: The lion of Judah ravished Israel
  and dispersed his sheep.

Jewish Prophet: Saul's descendants are fit to be
  keepers of flocks, but not of the people.

Samarian Prophet: The Lord of Israel shall reach
  you, and through me.

> (*Raises his staff against the Jewish
> Prophet.*)

Jewish Prophet: Lord, remember Your servant
  David.

(Raises a stone to cast at the Sumerian Prophet. Eleazar, a young prophet and singer, just come from Babylon, throws himself between the two.)

§

§

Eleazar: Refrain! Cover not with shame the names
 of Israel and Judah.

Samarian Prophet: Ah! is it you, prophet of shame?
 And how have you glorified Israel and Judah?

Jewish Prophet: Vile serpent, why came you from
 that nest? There is your God and your people,
 begone and glorify them!

First Levite: May the Lord vomit you out of His
 mouth, may your name disappear as spittle !

  (*The people gather round.*)

Second Levite: (*catching a harp from the willows*) I
 will break this cursed vessel.

Eleazar: (*catching his hand*) Touch not my harp, for
 it is innocent of my sins! Curse me, if you think I
 am worthy, but curse not the holy harp.

Third Levite: And how has it sanctified itself?

Eleazar: That never from the first rang a string
 insincerely.

A Boy: Aha ! Therefore you did hang it there.

Eleazar: (*to the Boy. Sadly*) Why, youth. say you so?

Boy: Don't pretend you do not understand!

An Old Man: This youth told you, Eleazar, what your conscience would have told you—but a mute cannot speak.

A Man: And it is a vanity to talk to the deaf. (*A child stretches out its arms to the harp.*)

The Child: Uncle, give me the toy.

First Mother: I told you, dare not to come to this man.

An Old Woman: (*to a girl standing near*) I see there is no more shame in Israel, when a girl stands uncovered and looks upon a traitor.

The Girl: But I...

First Woman: See, poor thing, it is a great woe when one cursed by God steals a girl's heart.

The Girl: If he be cursed, I also curse him. (*Veils herself and goes away.*)

§

§

Eleazar: (*to all*) Fathers and brothers, mothers and sisters, since when is it a custom among us to condemn without judging? Truly, clearly tell me, why am I become as a leper among you?

The Old Man: You became leprous in Babylon, singing for money in the courts to the sons of Baal.

Eleazar: Are you not all gathered here in Babylon for labor?

First Man: Laborers do not serve Moloch.

Eleazar: Whom then do their arms and vessels serve? Have they not built such an abode for Moloch, as never had our Lord in Jerusalem?

First Prophet: Taunt not captives with their slavery!

Eleazar: Am I not a captive? Why curse you me for my forced labor?

Second Prophet: The cord, the spade, the plow and axe in men's hands are men's slaves; but the word in a prophet's mouth must serve God only, and none other.

The Old Man: Yet will you ask for judgment, Eleazar?

Eleazar: I will, though the judgment end with stones. The Lord lives! You must judge by truth; an unjust curse shall turn against you.

§

§

The Old Man: Let us hear him. Let it not be said we
forsook truth on the ruins of Jerusalem. Tell us
what constrained you to sell the word.

Eleazar: That none bought my hands. My father
did not teach me to labor, and weak my mother
bred me. Though the harp obeys my hands,
neither plow nor axe obeys them. I fell under
a burden, and the overseer drove me from the
labor.

The Old Man: Let then your father and mother feed
you, who have not taught you to earn bread.

Eleazar: In Jerusalem I earned honorably by the
means they taught me, and here too—but the
bread burns that my father brings from Babylon;
hard it is to eat from a father's slavery.

First Levite: Not only bread your father brings, but
also golden rings.

Eleazar: (*to all*) Teach this Levite that gold burns,
and not only shines.

First Levite: (*slyly*) Why does your father's work
burn so?

Eleazar: Am I judged here, or my father? Bring
   then all fathers to judgment, that for their family
   lose their souls.

First Levite: Why did you not cry to the nation
   to feed you with the bread wherewith it feeds
   Levites and cripples?

Eleazar: I am not Levite nor cripple.

§

§

A Little Boy: (*to his father*) Daddy, give me bread!

The Father: I have none, my son.

A Man: Do you see? He heard talk of bread and
eating, and says too, "Give me bread."

Eleazar: Rightly says the boy. He answered for me
better than I could know. You all heard. While
in Israel they speak thus, Eleazar will not share
bread with Levites and cripples. He that has
bread, let him give to the child; I will take stones
from the captives. He that has fish, let him feed
the children, and give me a viper that drinks
blood from the heart. I shall take it and bear it
with me into the courts; it will give sting to my
words and its hissing they will hear in Babylon.

A Youth: Much will you earn for such songs in
Babylon! Surely less than you have earned for the
hymns of Zion.

Eleazar: Unwisely, boy, have you spoken. I sang
them not hymns of Zion. The hymn of Zion,
of all songs the ornament, was as a bride in
Jerusalem, as a wife in the holy city; here it were
as a concubine, for who takes a captive as a
lawful wife?

(The people sigh, Eleazar holds his peace and bows his head.)

§

§

A Man: Why did you not sing the songs of captivity? Why have you not poured the bitter tears of slavery? The cold drop pierces the stone—why would not hot tears touch even the wicked heart?

Eleazar: The Lord set pride in my soul. Never have I wept before strangers.

A Man: Pride befits not slaves.

First Prophet: The horn of pride in you rose above grief and holy love!

Eleazar: Measure not the measureless with the endless, for you will not see what will come of it.

A Youth: Eloquent is Eleazar among the captives! Why in the Babylonian courts do his love and grief and pride hold their peace? Surely the place is too small?

Eleazar: And did you think it were enough? Oh, youth, I have measured all those Babylonian courts and know their size. It happened I crossed that court where our people are building a tower for Moloch. I stopped and gazed at it. The marble is white as bones in the field, the porphyry grey as shed blood, the gold shines as a bright fire.

It stands unfinished, like ruins; the cries of our conquerors are heard, and the groans of our people. I know not how, with a great voice I shouted over the whole place, "Jerusalem!" With a cry answered the captives from the wall, and with laughter answered the guards. "Is that ruin called in any way, has that desert still a name?" I went away to the market where they sell captives into slavery. There a rich merchant was choosing the most lovely captives.

Women: Misery, misery, misery!

Eleazar: I said, "Think, lord, these girls have fathers and brothers. Were your sister or daughter taken captive, would the foe sell her?" He answered, "It's the fate of captives." I went farther and saw a small, weak slave, and a tall, strong Babylonian loaded him with wares, as a mule, and drove him with a stick. I cried, "Stay! To torment such a small boy!" "For this he is a slave," he answered, arrogant. "And were your son sold," said I, "he too would be a slave?" "Surely; not otherwise," said the rich man, and laughed aloud, "but I do not sell my sons, and yours, you see, I buy." Who, what will touch such hearts? Once only with my songs I got a tear from a stranger; the king himself wept at the end of Saul and Jonathan's death.

A Voice from the People: Long live the merciful king! In him only is our hope..

§

§

Eleazar: The merciful king wished to reward me
   generously.

First Levite: What gave he you, Eleazar?

Eleazar: He gave me a chamber in his palace and
   Jewish captives, as many as I would. From that
   moment I cursed the songs that get tears from
   conquerors; they are the tears of the Nile's
   crocodiles.

The Youth: You should have sung them of the
   fame of our ancestors, that they might know the
   strength of our people.

Eleazar: I sang.

The Youth: And what?

   (*Eleazar is silent.*)

§

§

The Old Man: Say, Eleazar, how the strangers heard
the songs of fame.

Eleazar: (*slowly*) One of them whistled and,
smiling, shook his head. Another said, "Not all
that is true." A third bade me join the military
singers; and all, one after the other, said, "Is there
only that in the world which is in Jerusalem?
Know you no songs of Edom, of Misraim? Was
not the fame of Amalek, Ammon and Amareus
as the past fame of Israel?"

First Prophet: O Lord, chastise the hostile lips with
the dumbness of death.

Eleazar: I began to sing them of Edom, of Misraim,
of foreign speeches in a foreign speech. They
heard how treacherous Edom's crooked sword
broke against Ashur's armor; how Amalek,
Ammon and Amareus from ravishers became
slaves; how Misraim, master of half the world,
once the lord of the tribes of Israel, had to
submit to the eternal might; how horse and rider
fell into the sea, and all the Pharaoh's might,
when it was voided the abhorred house of toil
and the cursed place of slavery was devastated.

The Youth: And what did the listeners?

Eleazar: There were those who paled.

Second Prophet: May they grow pale and cold for ever!

The Youth: Why did you not say that also for these will come a day of judgment?

Eleazar: For that word there is no room in Babylon! Today I sang them of Ophir, Sidon and Tyre, their power and wisdom and treasures, as are not and never will be in the Babylonian treasuries.

First Levite: Did you gain much for this song?

Eleazar: Think you, the treasures of Canaan? See, I have bread for this day's supper.

The Youth: Surely, for songs that praised Babylon's power you have earned more than one golden ring?

§

§

Eleazar: The vile speaks only with poison, but poison hurts not every man. When have you heard me sing songs of the Babylonian glory and might? (*The youth is silent and ashamed.*) You have judged yourself by your silence.

The Old Man: Eleazar, it may be your songs are good in Babylon, but Misraim and Edom and all their tongues will not bring Palestine to mind and awake the thought of Jerusalem.

Eleazar: Is there already need to bring it to our minds?

The Old Man: Not to us, but to those that among foes have used to speak the foreign speech.

Eleazar: How will they understand the inborn song? How sing it in a foreign speech?

The Old Man: With your foreign words you will forget to say, "Jerusalem!"

§

§

*(Eleazar stands thoughtfully. His hand
begins to touch the strings of his harp,
and his voice sounds, neither singing, nor
wailing, as of one who sleeps.)*

Eleazar: My right hand was strong;
who could overcome it?
Did I then say to myself:
"Happy am I; I have my right arm?"
Spoke I ever thus:
"Right arm, know you are mine!"
But the evil foe wounded my hand
and cut off my right arm.
Whom shall I overcome now?
Who will not overcome me?
Day and night I say to myself,
"Oh, misery, where is my hand?"
I look upon my shoulder and weep,
"Right arm, how forget you?"

*(He quietly touches the strings. The
people weep.)*

My father had a rich vineyard,
my mother a green garden.
I walked in it, plucked the berries
and trampled the leaves with my feet.
An evil neighbor set fire to our vineyard

and wasted the green garden.
The vine was burned, the berries dropped
and its glorious beauty fell to ashes.
If I find beneath my feet, be it only one leaf,
I shall press it to my heart.
Dear brothers, say, has none of you,
be it only one leaf from my vine?

> (*The strings sound still more sadly, and
> the weeping becomes louder.*)

I dreamed a dread dream—who shall divine it?
'Twas as if I fell into the hands of the enemies.
What have they done to me, my terrible enemies?
My arms still are mighty, my legs still are strong,
my eyes still are clear, and my body is not hurt.
Only my tongue, my tongue was for their vengeance.
I wished to speak a word; I wished to lift up my voice.
But my lips spoke with blood and cried with silence.

> (*A long pause. The harp falls from
> Eleazar's hands and the sigh of its strings
> dies away. The people's cries cease
> abruptly. Silence. He speaks with respect,
> but firmly and distinctly.*)

Fathers and brothers, mothers and sisters!
I wait for a stone or a word from you. (*Silence*)
What curse is more awful than silence?

§

§

The Old Man: We do not curse you, Eleazar.

The Youth: Forgive me my hard word, brother.

Eleazar: You do not curse me. I forgive all your
  words. But still I am cursed with the dreadful
  curse of blood. The blood of our fathers, shed
  in vain for our lost liberty, weighs upon my
  head and yours, and bows down our forehead
  to the earth, to the stone that the hand of my
  people hurled not against me. A man's son fell
  and cut himself on a sharp stone; in despair he
  rent his garments of honor and strewed ashes of
  disgrace upon his head. Oh, as the temple I fell,
  as Jerusalem we fell all, and, as hard as it is to
  rebuild our temple, so hard it is for us to rise out
  of the dust of slavery's dishonor.

  Shame fell upon our arms that rose not to take
  the lives of us conquered, but rose to labor for
  the enemies. Leprosy covered the bodies of the
  girls of Zion, that they drowned not themselves
  in the Euphrates, but went to entertain the sons
  of lasciviousness and nurse the fruit of their
  shame. And shame covered my lips that from
  hunger these lips grew not still, but spoke the
  strange speech in those cursed courts where all
  songs sound—and only that which bursts from

the heart must die. Infamy oppresses us worse than chains, it bites worse than iron fetters. To suffer chains is inhuman shame, to forget them unbroken yet greater ignominy. Two paths we have, death or disgrace, till we find a way to Jerusalem. Brothers, let us look for a way to the temple as the gazelle seeks water in the desert, that the mighty foe may not say, "Now have I slain Israel; it is dead!" And before we find it, let us fight for our life as the wounded badger in the hunt; let it not be said among men, "The Lord of Israel fell asleep in Heaven." Oh, Babylon, too early is it to rejoice!

Still our harps sound among the willows, still tears flow into the Babylonian rivers, still the daughter of Zion burns with shame, still the lion of Judah roars with fury. The Lord lives, my soul lives, Israel lives, even in Babylon!

§

§

The Voice of an Overseer from the Camp: To the
tents, Israel; the night comes.

> (*The people separate and go to their*
> *tents. On the distant towers are seen*
> *the Babylonian magicians, foretelling*
> *from the stars. The camp grows still.*
> *From Babylon faintly comes the sound*
> *of revels. The solemn night trembles*
> *over the captive camp and Babylon. Here*
> *and there quicken the Overseers' fires.*
> *Silence.*)

(*Curtain*)

www.ingramcontent.com/pod-product-compliance
Lightning Source LLC
Chambersburg PA
CBHW020448030426
42337CB00014B/1453